TALK ABOUT
Bullying

Jane Bingham

WAYLAND

First published in 2008 by Wayland

Copyright © Wayland 2008

Wayland
338 Euston Road
London NW1 3BH

Wayland Australia
Level 17/207 Kent Street
Sydney, NSW 2000

Editor: Camilla Lloyd
Consultant: Jayne Wright
Designer: Tim Mayer
Picture researcher: Kathy Lockley

Picture acknowledgments: The author and publisher would like to thank the following for allowing their pictures to be reproduced in this publication: Cover photograph: Image Source/Corbis. Alain Nogues/Corbis: 45B; Bubbles Photolibrary/Alamy: 7, 27; Christina Kennedy/Getty Images: 17; ColorBlind Images/Iconica/Getty Images: 5, 34; Corbis: 33TC; David Anthony/Alamy: 10-11T bkg., 22-23T bkg., 32-33T bkg., 36-37T bkg., 38, 43T bkg., 44-45T bkg.; David J Green - Lifestyle/Alamy: 13, 32B; Digital Vision: 10 T; Gideon Mendel/Corbis: 41; Heide Benser/zefa/Corbis: 18B; Image Source/Corbis: 21; Isopix/Rex Features: 18-19; John Birdsall Social Issues Photo Library: 9, 24-25, 30; John Powell Photographer/Alamy: 1, 4; Mark Phillips/Alamy: 8; Martin Ruetschi/Keystone/Corbis: 28-29; Nick Daly/Stone/Getty Images: 16; Ole Graf/zefa/Corbis: 31; Peter Andrews/Corbis: 20; Phanie Agency/Rex Features: 42; Randy Faris/Corbis: 26; Richard Levine/Alamy: 39; Thinkstock/Corbis: 22TL, 23B, 35; vario images GmbH & Co. KG/Alamy: 12, 36B; Vehbi Koca/Alamy: 44; Voisin/Phanie/Rex Features: 40.

Sources:
NSPCC website (4)
BBC: www.bbc.co.uk (9)
Source: Survey by the UK Association of Teachers and Lecturers (13)
The Guardian (23)

British Library Cataloguing in Publication Data:
Bingham, Jane
   Talk about bullying
   1. Bullying - Juvenile literature
   I. Title II. Bullying
   302.3

ISBN: 978 0 7502 4617 0

Printed in China

Wayland is a division of Hachette Children's Books, an Hachette Livre UK Company
www.hachettelivre.co.uk

CONTENTS

Chapter 1

Let's talk about bullying

People have been whispering behind your back for months. You keep getting nasty messages on your phone. The gang of kids who were mean to you last week are threatening to beat you up . . . These are all types of bullying, and they are all frightening and upsetting. Nobody should have to suffer bullying, but what exactly can be done about it?

A serious problem

Bullying involves being singled out and teased or mistreated over a period of time. It is one of the biggest problems faced by young people. Bullying often takes place in school, but some boys and girls have to deal with bullies on the streets, in sports and leisure clubs, and even at home. Many bullies also use mobile phones and the Internet to torment their victims. This makes targets feel that there is no escape from the bullying.

When young people have to cope with persistent bullying, they can become seriously depressed.

Being bullied makes people feel vulnerable, angry and miserable. Some targets of bullying stay away from school, just to get away from the bullies. A few become so desperate that they even turn to suicide. Sadly, many young people try to cope with bullying on their own, even though there is lots of help and support available.

4

Sometimes bullying involves cutting someone out of all the jokes and fun.

Looking at bullying

This book takes a careful look at bullying. It describes what happens when a young person is bullied and how it feels to be bullied. It examines the reasons why people become bullies and considers ways of challenging bullying. Finally, the book looks at bullying in the wider world, and asks the question – what can be done to put a stop to bullying?

FACTS

* ✳ **In a survey of pupils in the UK aged 9 to 10, over half reported that they had been bullied during the previous term.**

* ✳ **Around a third of boys and a quarter of girls admitted that they had bullied other children.**

* ✳ **A survey of pupils aged 10 to 14 found that over a quarter of pupils who had been bullied had kept it secret.**

Chapter 2

What is bullying?

Bullying can take many forms. Often bullies make fun of people or make them feel unwanted. Sometimes they steal or damage personal possessions. Some bullies use violent behaviour, or threats of violence. But whatever form bullying takes, it always has the same result. Bullies make their targets feel lonely, depressed, angry and afraid.

Teasing and taunting

One of the main ways that bullies make others feel bad is by making fun of them. Bullies taunt their targets by laughing at them, calling them names, and imitating them. Sometimes, a bully will try to make another child look ridiculous by playing cruel practical jokes.

When bullies decide to make someone a target, they look for something to pick on. This can be a person's race or religion, the clothes they wear, or even the colour of their hair. Once a bully has decided to victimize somebody, he or she will always find something to make fun of.

It happened to me

Sam was a friendly boy who enjoyed computer games and playing football. He had always had plenty of friends, but when he was 10 years old his family moved to a different part of the country. Sam thought he would soon settle into his new school, but it wasn't easy. Some of the boys decided they didn't want him around. They laughed at the way he talked, and even made fun of his curly hair. Sam was very hurt and angry. He didn't understand why the bullies wouldn't give him a chance.

Out in the cold

Some bullies take deliberate steps to make their targets feel rejected. They make it very clear that a certain person is unwanted, and 'freeze them out' of any activities. When young people are treated like this, they can feel very lonely. They can even start to believe that there is something seriously wrong with them. Bullying can damage the victims' self-esteem, making them lose confidence and belief in themselves.

When everybody seems to be against you, it's easy to start feeling bad about yourself.

Cruel messages

Bullies often send cruel messages to their targets. In the past, bullies used to send written notes, but now they usually send text messages, instant messages or e-mails. They may post nasty comments or embarrassing pictures on the Internet. Bullies today also target people in chatrooms, sending sarcastic messages and making them look bad in front of all the other people in the room. This kind of bullying, using new technology, is sometimes known as cyberbullying.

In the media

In September 2007, schoolgirl Julianne Flory began to receive insulting and threatening messages posted on her web page and on her instant messaging service. One message threatened the safety of Julianne and her family. *'They said they were going to get me tomorrow and I was going to be stabbed and my brothers and mum and dad would be hurt.'* Julianne printed out the message and took it to her father. *'He started shaking and crying,'* she remembers. *'Then we went to the police.'* The police managed to track the bullies down and used harassment orders to keep them away from Julianne and her family.

When bullies can even reach you on your home computer, you can feel that nowhere is safe.

No escape

Cyberbullying doesn't stop when school ends or even in the school holidays. Using new technology, bullies can pursue their targets wherever they go. Some boys and girls receive threatening messages every time they turn on their phone or their computer. This can be a very frightening experience. They can feel that there is nowhere to escape from their tormentors.

Spreading lies

It is very common for bullies to spread untrue stories about their targets. They may deliberately start rumours at school, or they may post hurtful stories on the Internet.

Bullies may also try to get their targets into trouble by sending out false messages. Once the lies and stories have started to spread, it can be very hard to prove that they are untrue.

If you are being targeted by cyberbullies, simply answering your phone can become a terrifying ordeal.

Some targets of bullying can suddenly discover that all their old friends have turned against them.

No more friends

Bullies often try to isolate their targets by turning all their old friends against them. The bullies may spread lies about a certain person. Or they may frighten other young people and make them join in with the bullying. Gradually, a boy or girl can start to feel that they are left to face the bullies alone. This can make them feel very lonely, isolated and betrayed.

Sometimes bullies steal your personal possessions. This can be a scary and upsetting experience.

Nothing is safe

Some bullies start a deliberate campaign of stealing or damaging personal possessions. This can make their targets feel that nothing they own is safe. Bullies may steal money or something valuable. They may damage a favourite possession, or they may concentrate on a person's schoolbooks. For example, some bullies deliberately 'lose' an important exercise book. When this happens, targets of bullying can get into lots of trouble at home and at school.

Making threats

Many bullies frighten other children with threats of violence or with other awful punishments. They may warn their targets that terrible things will happen to them if they dare to tell anyone that they are being bullied. Often the bullies don't say exactly what will happen to their targets. Instead they just leave them to imagine the worst. This can be a terrifying experience, as a young person lies awake at night wondering what might happen next.

TALK ABOUT

Look at these statements about bullying. Do you agree or disagree with them?

✳ Bullying is a fact of life and has always happened.

✳ Targets of bullying should just deal with it and not make a fuss.

✳ Bullying causes a great deal of suffering and should always be challenged.

✳ It is important for both the bully and the target that the situation is dealt with very quickly.

✳ Bullying should always be taken seriously.

For advice on how to extend Talk About discussions please see the Notes for Teachers on page 47.

Physical violence

Bullying often involves some kind of violence. In many cases, the violence is apparently 'minor', such as shoving, kicking or punching. But this does not mean that it is OK. All kinds of violence are wrong and should be stopped. Even 'minor' physical violence can be deeply frightening and humiliating.

Many young people live in fear of a violent attack like this.

FACTS

The figures below reveal how violence is a serious problem in schools.

✳ Over a quarter of UK pupils have been threatened with violence by other pupils.

✳ More than 1 in 10 school pupils have been physically attacked at school.

✳ Around 1 in 10 pupils say they have missed school because of their fear of violence.

✳ Almost 1 in 5 pupils in the USA have been threatened with violence by other pupils.

When violence is recorded on camera, it is known as 'happy slapping'. Happy slapping is on the increase among boys and girls.

Girls and violence

Recently there has been a dramatic growth in the number of cases of girls who are using violence. Girls often use less obvious forms of violence, such as pinching or hair-pulling. Some of them also take part in the growing trend of 'happy slapping'. This involves any form of violence that is filmed on a mobile phone camera and distributed to others. Some people try to defend 'happy slapping' as 'a bit of harmless fun', but it is really just an excuse for physical cruelty.

Serious violence

In rare cases, bullying can involve serious violence and victims are beaten up or even killed. Knife crime is on the increase everywhere, and some schools have begun to check that their students are not carrying knives in school. In the UK and the USA, there have even been some terrible examples of students using guns. Carrying a weapon, even for self-defence, can have awful consequences and the weapon can be snatched and used against you.

Chapter 3

How does it feel to be bullied?

When people realize that they are being bullied, they can experience a range of emotions. Often they feel frightened and alone, and sometimes they feel angry. Being bullied can also make people feel worthless and ashamed. In a few tragic cases, targets of bullying can take the terrible decision to kill themselves.

Scared and alone

Most people who experience bullying feel afraid. They may be scared because the bully is hurting them or making threats. Or they may simply feel frightened of the unknown. It can be terrifying not knowing what you are going to face when you go into school or when you switch on your phone.

In this situation, some young people feel that they can no longer face their tormentors. They start to stay away from school and avoid social occasions. Unfortunately, this can lead to many other problems, as pupils start to fall behind in their schoolwork and become isolated and lonely.

Ill and depressed

It is very common for people who are bullied to become ill. Victims of bullies often suffer from sleeplessness and panic attacks. Some people stop eating properly and others try to comfort themselves by eating too much. Many people who are faced with bullies become depressed, and some experience a complete breakdown. People who are made ill by bullying need professional support to help them recover.

In the media

In April 2007, 13-year-old Casey Knibbs was found hanged at his home, after receiving taunts and threats from four other pupils on a popular teenage chat site. The mother of one of the pupils at Casey's school said: *'It is absolutely tragic – parents need to be aware of what is happening on these websites.'* She added that, *'My daughter told me that Casey never said a word to anyone about it – until it was too late.'*

Being bullied makes you feel scared and lonely. But it can make all the difference if someone is there to comfort you.

It's natural to feel angry when you are being bullied, but if you control your anger you will show the bullies that they can't get to you.

Feeling angry

Some people react to being bullied with feelings of rage. They feel very angry about their cruel treatment, especially as they have done nothing to deserve it. However, when targets respond violently it can lead to trouble. They can be seen by others as behaving just as badly as the bully. They can even be punished in the same way, even though this seems unfair.

When people live with pent-up feelings of anger, they can make themselves really ill. It is very important to find a way to let out these feelings. Many people find that taking physical exercise helps them to feel calmer. Some feel better after they have written down their feelings. But the best way of all to deal with angry feelings is to talk to someone who understands.

Family troubles

It is very common for young people to try to deal with the problem of bullying on their own. But this can have a negative effect on their life at home. Young people who are trying to cope with bullying often become withdrawn and no longer take much part in family life. They may also become moody and irritable. Sometimes parents react to this new behaviour by becoming angry too.

Just at a time when they really need support, young people can find they are having constant rows at home. This is very tough on everyone in the family.

*Being bullied makes you feel on edge all the time –
and this can easily lead to arguments at home.*

It happened to me

Over the past few months, some girls at school had started to pick on Amy.
They said her clothes were old-fashioned and they made her look stupid. Amy
felt angry and humiliated. She begged her mother to buy her some new clothes,
but her mum said she couldn't afford it. Amy was furious with her mum, but she
couldn't tell her why. She had to keep her secret about the bullying to herself.
Amy felt hurt and angry all the time. She felt that everyone was against her –
even her mum.

Feeling worthless

When people are being bullied, it's very easy for them to start to believe the things the bullies say. They may feel worthless, and even blame themselves for the bullying. Once a boy or girl starts to feel like this, he or she can rapidly lose confidence and start to look frightened and depressed. Sadly, these reactions make the young person even more likely to be picked on by bullies.

Self-harm

Some targets of bullies feel so bad about themselves that they are driven to self-harm. Cutting and other forms of self-harm are signs of extreme distress. When young people practice self-harm, they are sending out a clear cry for help, and they are in urgent need of expert help.

Persistent bullying can eat away at your confidence, leaving you feeling hopeless and depressed.

Suicide

A few victims of bullying become so desperate that they decide they cannot bear the bullying any longer. Sadly, they do not realize that there are lots of people who can help, and they see death as the only way out. Today, there are some tragic cases of suicides caused by bullying. However, there are also organizations that can help when people are driven to thoughts of suicide. See page 47 for information about where to get help.

In a few tragic cases, the bullying becomes so extreme that suicide seems the only possible option.

It happened to me

When he was 11 years old, Nathan almost succeeded in killing himself. Fortunately, his mum discovered him just in time. He had been bullied for three years and he felt completely isolated and alone. After Nathan's suicide attempt, the truth about the bullying came out, and two of the bullies were excluded from school. The other students were really shocked by what had happened. They realized they should have given Nathan more support and were very relieved to see him back at school again. Now Nathan has a good group of friends and he has lots of things to look forward to, but he never forgets how close he came to ending his life.

Chapter 4

Who gets bullied?

Anyone can be a target for bullies – and some famous people were bullied when they were young. Miss Dynamite, Johnny Depp and David Beckham were all picked on by bullies when they were at school. If a person is being bullied, it does not mean there is something wrong with them. The people being bullied don't necessarily need to change, but those carrrying out the bullying do.

Any excuse

Bullies can choose anything to pick on. They may target a girl or boy because of their race or religion, because they have freckles or wear glasses, or because of the clothes they wear. Sometimes bullies choose targets who are very good looking because the bullies are jealous. Of course, none of these reasons for bullying makes sense. They are just excuses to make the bullies feel better about themselves.

When he was at school, Johnny Depp was picked on by other kids. They thought he was a 'freak' because he liked to play on his own.

Some young people are singled out for bullying just because they are clever and do well at school.

Picking on differences

Sometimes children are targeted by bullies because they stand out from the crowd. These individuals may not be interested in exactly the same things as everybody else. They may not follow fashion or modern music. They may not be good at sport, or they may want to work hard at school. These girls and boys are often labelled as 'freaks' and 'geeks', and they can be given a very hard time.

TALK ABOUT

Some people think it is important to follow the latest trends. They say that if young people want to have friends they need to keep up with the latest music and wear fashionable clothes.

Other people think these things are not important. They say it is good for people to be individual. They also say that people should dress how they want and listen to the music they really like.

✳ Do you think it's OK to be different?

Racism is one of the cruellest forms of bullying. It is also against the law.

Racist bullying

Some bullies decide to target people because of their race, colour or religion. They may call their targets insulting names and mock their religion. They may also taunt young people of other races about the clothes they wear or the food they eat. In some cases bullies even tell these people that they are not wanted and that they should return to their own country. This kind of bullying is known as racism and it is against the law. Nobody should have to put up with racist bullying.

In the
media

SHARP RISE IN PUPILS SUSPENDED FOR RACISM

In April 2007, a report in *The Guardian* announced that the number of UK pupils suspended from school for racist abuse had risen by nearly one-third in a year. One quarter of all the suspensions were due to physical attacks on other pupils or staff. A spokesperson for the Commission for Racial Equality said: *'These figures suggest that something is going seriously wrong. Worryingly, racism is a learned behaviour – these kids are not born racists.'* The spokesperson added, *'We owe it to every child to ensure that they can study and develop their abilities in a safe environment.'*

Taunts about weight

Boys and girls who are overweight are often picked on by bullies. This cruel treatment can make them feel terrible about themselves. Faced with taunts about their weight, some young people take comfort in eating more. They can enter into a vicious cycle, when they eat to make themselves feel better, but this makes them the target of more bullying. Others take the decision to change the way they look by going on a very strict diet. Some young teenagers go on to develop an eating disorder, such as anorexia, as a result of bullying about their weight.

If you are already self-conscious about your weight, bullying can make you feel very depressed.

Homophobic bullying

Recently, there has been a great increase in homophobic bullying in schools. Homophobia is a hatred of homosexuals and of anything associated with being 'gay'. Homophobic bullies single out boys and girls who are homosexual or who are believed to be homosexual, and treat them very cruelly. Bullies can make their targets' lives a misery with their taunts and threats.

Homophobic bullies don't just target people who are homosexual. Boys who are not particularly 'macho' or sporty are often labelled as 'gay' and bullies use the term 'gay' as a general term of abuse. This kind of hatred and name-calling can be very hurtful, especially to young people with gay parents. It is also very frightening for young people who are struggling with their emerging sexuality.

It happened to me

Nick was always being picked on by other boys and called cruel names. They seemed to turn against him just because he was small for his age and didn't like playing football. The bullies called him 'gayboy' and laughed behind his back and ran away from him whenever he came near.

Nick was very upset and frightened. He'd never thought about it before, but perhaps he was gay? And if he were gay, would people treat him like this for the rest of his life? Nick couldn't bear the thought of what lay ahead of him. He felt there was no way out, and he even thought about killing himself.

Some bullies make a point of not including people with disabilities in their games. But just because people have a disability, it doesn't mean they cannot enjoy sport too.
(This photograph has been staged and no one in it has suffered from or been involved in bullying.)

Picking on disabilities

Bullies often pick on people with disabilities. They may target someone with a physical disability and make cruel remarks about them or exclude them from their games. Sometimes they may pick on people with learning difficulties, and try to make them look stupid in front of the other children. When young people have a disability, they already have a lot of challenges to deal with, so being attacked by bullies is especially hard to bear.

25

Chapter 5

Why do people bully?

One of the main reasons for bullying is fear. Most bullies have had some bad experiences in their past, and they have learned not to trust other people. Often, they feel threatened by others, especially those who seem different to them. When bullies try to frighten other people, they feel that they are in control.

Children learn what they live. If they have been bullied at home, they often become bullies themselves.

Learning bullying

Sadly, many young bullies learn their negative behaviour at home. Often they have an older sibling, parent or step-parent, or some other adult in their life, who treats them in a cruel or mocking way. Some young people who grow up to be bullies have also suffered physical violence at home. These children grow up thinking that the way to gain power over others is to bully them. When they get to school, they try out the same behaviour on other children.

Mixed feelings

Many young bullies spend a lot of time feeling frightened. They can feel that their life at home is out of control. So it's not surprising that they try to take control in other parts of their life. Often bullies feel that if they can make somebody else feel scared, they will finally be in charge.

Picking on other people may make a bully feel better for a short time, but bullies soon discover that they still feel unhappy about themselves. Some of them even realize that they are copying the kind of behaviour that they hate. These young people need expert help to overcome their problems. You can read more about how to prevent bullying behaviour on pages 40-41.

A child being bullied by parents, brothers or sisters in the home may learn from his or her experiences that bullying is acceptable and that it is all right to hurt others.

TALK ABOUT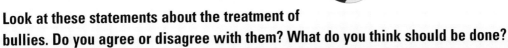

Look at these statements about the treatment of bullies. Do you agree or disagree with them? What do you think should be done?

✳ Bullies should face very hard punishments. They have made their victims suffer so they should suffer too.

✳ Bullies should be treated with understanding as they might have been victims once themselves.

✳ It's important to understand why bullies behave the way they do.

Going with the gang

Bullies don't just learn about bullying at home.
They can also be influenced by other young people.
They may be part of a gang where everybody takes
part in bullying. Today, there are growing numbers
of gangs whose members deliberately persecute
their victims.

Once a young person has become part of a gang,
things can rapidly get out of hand. It can be very hard –
and frightening — to stand up against the other gang
members and say that their behaviour is wrong.

*When young people get
together in gangs, they
sometimes do cruel things
they would never do alone.*

Adult examples

Often young bullies learn their aggressive behaviour from the things they see in the adult world. They may hear people making racist or homophobic comments. Or they may see scenes of violence and bullying in films and on TV. These examples can make young people believe it is perfectly normal to be cruel to others.

Adult bullies

Not all bullies are young. Adult bullies can target young people, threatening violence and forcing them to do things they don't want to do. In some very frightening cases, adults may be violently abusive.

Adult bullies often pick on boys and girls in their own family, or in a family they know. But there are also cases of teachers, sports coaches and youth leaders who bully young people. When boys and girls are faced with adult bullies they can feel helpless and terrified, and it is essential that they find help. Turn to page 47 for a list of people and places to contact.

It happened to me

Luke was part of a gang at school. At first he felt proud to be one of the 'hard' kids, but then he realized some nasty things were going on. The gang was targetting other pupils and making their lives a misery. Luke decided he had to do something. He told the others that what they were doing was wrong, and he wasn't going to get involved with any more bullying. Luke thought everyone would turn on him, but he was amazed. Most of the gang agreed with what he was saying, but they hadn't dared to say so themselves.

Chapter 6

Beating bullying

Fortunately there are ways of challenging and stopping bullying. This chapter gives advice on how to cope with being bullied and where to go for help. It outlines what to do if you have a friend who is being bullied. It also describes how bullies can be helped to overcome their problems.

Finding help

If you are being bullied, the most important thing to do is to find help. Bullying isn't a guilty secret that should be kept to yourself.

Talking things over with someone who cares can make you feel much better about yourself.

It is very helpful to have a clear account of how you have been bullied. Try to keep a record with dates and times and brief details about what happened to you.

Bullying is always wrong and it needs to be stopped. If you are being bullied, you need to talk to an adult who you can trust. This could be your mum or dad, a teacher, a school counsellor, or your doctor. Sometimes you'll need to try more than one person before you find the right one, but you shouldn't give up. You have a right to be helped and you should never have to put up with being bullied.

Preparing to tell

Once you have decided to talk to a teacher, pick a quiet time when they are on their own. You may find it easier to write down what you want to say in a letter and give it to your teacher first. Some schools have a system where students can put a note in a box, or send an e-mail or a text. It can also help if you come prepared with something written down, such as a record of the times when you were bullied, and what exactly was done and said.

TALK ABOUT

Some people say that telling tales is wrong. They call it 'grassing' or 'running to the teacher'. They also claim that if you leave things alone, the problem will eventually go away.

Other people disagree. They say it's always better to have things out in the open. Then the person being bullied can stop feeling afraid, and the bully can get help too.

✳ Do you think it is wrong to tell people about bullying?

Helplines and websites

Some young people find it very hard to talk to anyone around them. But there are still plenty of places to go for help. There are telephone helplines that you can call 24 hours a day, whenever you need support or advice. Helplines such as ChildLine are staffed by friendly, sympathetic staff who will listen carefully to your problems and give you expert advice on what to do next.

There are also some excellent websites that provide clear advice on how to cope with bullying. Most websites have real-life accounts of how other young people have dealt with bullies. You can find out more about helplines and websites on page 47.

When life gets really hard, it's comforting to know that you can call a helpline for support.

Today, cyberbullying is growing fast, but there are some simple ways to help stay safe online (see page 37).

Staying safe

If you are being bullied, it is very important to keep yourself safe. There are several commonsense steps you can take to look after yourself. Make sure you're not alone at breaktimes and lunchtimes, and make arrangements to travel to school with other children. There are also ways to protect yourself from cyberbullying. Turn to page 37 for a list of actions you can take to stop the cyberbullies.

It happened to me

Aisha had been putting up with bullying for months. People at school called her racist names and made cruel comments about her family. Aisha didn't want to worry her parents, but she was desperate to talk to somebody. So, in the end, she decided to call a helpline. As soon as she started to speak to the counsellor, Aisha felt more relaxed. She knew she had found someone who really understood what she was going through.

The counsellor helped Aisha understand how she could tackle the problem herself. She also suggested ways that Aisha could talk to her parents about her worries. After the phone call, Aisha felt much stronger and more able to deal with the bullying. She also felt that she was no longer alone. She could always ring the helpline again.

Positive signs

Most bullies are trying to get a reaction. They want to see their targets getting upset, or looking frightened or miserable. In this situation, the best thing you can do is show the bullies that their actions don't bother you. Once they realize they are getting no reaction, there is a very good chance that they will go away.

Body language is very important. If you look timid and frightened, the bullies will probably pick on you even more. But if you hold your head up and look cheerful, you will send out a very different message. Even if you don't feel confident inside, try to stand tall and look unafraid. It will show the bullies that you're perfectly happy with the way you are. Then they will probably decide that it isn't worth picking on you.

If you walk tall and look the bullies in the face, you will find that they show much less interest in you.

Don't let the bullies get to you

Bullies want to make their targets miserable, but this is not a reason for them to succeed. If you start believing the horrible things they say, you are just letting them win.

Keep reminding yourself of all the things that are good about you. Be kind to yourself, and don't stop doing the things you enjoy. Even if you don't feel very sociable, try not to lose contact with your friends. Friends can support you, listen to your worries and give you more confidence.

Even if you are feeling down, try not to cut yourself off from your friends. They can be a great comfort and support.

DOs & DON'Ts

✳ **Try to stay cool and keep your temper.**

✳ **Ask a trusted adult to help put a stop to the problem.**

✳ **Take some simple steps to keep yourself safe.**

✳ **Keep a diary of what's happening to you.**

✳ **Visit a website or phone a helpline for advice and support.**

✳ **Never bottle up your feelings.**

✳ **Don't let the bullies stop you feeling good about yourself.**

✳ **Don't think that there is anything wrong with you. The bullies are the ones who are in the wrong.**

Keeping cool

When you are being bullied, it is very easy to lose your temper. Sometimes people respond to bullying by shouting back or getting involved in a fight. This is always a bad idea, as it can very quickly lead to more violence. If you are caught being violent or verbally abusive, a teacher will find it difficult to believe your version of events.

Even if you feel furious inside, you should try your best to keep cool. Instead of responding straightaway, give yourself some time to calm down. Then walk away as calmly as you can, and ignore the bullies. Remember, the bullies want to see you get upset. So, when you stay cool, you are refusing to let them take control.

It's very hard to stay cool when you are faced with bullies, but if you lose your temper, the bullies will feel they've won.

Stop the cyberbullies

Some people think that there is nothing you can do to stop cyberbullying. But this is not true. Mobile phone companies and Internet Service Providers (ISPs) can trace bullies, and you shouldn't be afraid to report them.

If you are threatened with violence by a cyberbully, you can report the threats to the police. You can also take steps to protect yourself when you are using your computer or your phone. Look at the panel below for advice on staying safe in cyberspace.

DOs & DON'Ts

✳ **Save any bullying emails, text messages or images. Then show them to someone you can trust.**

✳ **Note the time and date that the messages were sent, plus any details you have about the sender. This information can be used to trace the bullies.**

✳ **If you are being bullied on instant messenger, in a chatroom or on a social networking site, report it immediately to the website administrators. (You should be able to do this through the sites.)**

✳ **Block instant messages from certain people or use mail filters to block e-mails from specific e-mail addresses.**

✳ **If you are being bullied, don't keep the same mobile phone number, and only give your new number to close friends.**

✳ **Don't keep quiet about threats from cyberbullies. Always tell the police about threats of violence.**

Schools against bullying

Most schools have a strict anti-bullying policy. These policies set out clear guidelines on the kind of behaviour that is unacceptable. Pupils who ignore these guidlines can expect to face severe punishments. Bullies can be suspended or even excluded from school.

Many schools take part in an anti-bullying week. They hold meetings and workshops about bullying and sell wristbands to raise people's awareness of the problem.

Many schools have a school council where pupils can discuss issues that concern them, such as bullying. Some schools also run anti-bullying campaigns. They organize bullying awareness sessions and put up posters around the school to make everyone aware that bullying will not be tolerated. The people involved in anti-bullying in the schools also make sure that anyone being bullied knows exactly where to go for help.

Do you know what your school does to challenge bullying? If you think that not enough is being done, you could start an anti-bullying campaign.

TALK ABOUT

Some people say that if you notice someone being bullied, you should not get involved. They claim there is nothing useful you can do. Other people disagree. They say you should always try to put a stop to bullying. They believe that when you let bullying happen, you are actively encouraging it.

✳ If you know or have a suspicion that someone is being bullied, is it your problem or not? Can you help?

Watching out for bullies

What can you do if you notice that someone is being bullied? It's clearly not a good idea to get involved in a dangerous situation, but there are still things you can do to help.

If you know the person who is being bullied, you should encourage them to ask for help. In some cases, you may decide that you should talk to a trusted adult, even if the person being bullied doesn't want to tell.

Making a difference

Sometimes it is necessary to take action to change people's attitudes. These girls are protesting against a computer game, in which the players take on the role of a school bully.

When someone is being bullied, they really need a friend. If you listen to them and give them your support, you will make them feel much better about themselves. If the bullies are your friends, you should also think about talking to them. It takes courage to speak out against bullying, but it can make a difference. You may be able to make people think again about their actions, and save others from being hurt.

Bullies need help too

Young people who are caught bullying can face some very serious punishments. However, punishment is only part of the way that bullying is dealt with in schools and society. Bullies need to recognize the harm they are causing, and make a deliberate decision to change their behaviour. In some cases, they will need expert help to encourage them to make a positive change.

Sources of help

Many bullies feel afraid to seek help. They are scared that people will judge them and they will get into even more trouble. However, this needn't be the case. There are plenty of people who can help and support young people who get involved in bullying. Experienced counsellors can help bullies understand the causes of their behaviour and work with them to change their attitudes.

If a young person wants help, they can contact their school counsellor in confidence. Or they may prefer to ring a telephone helpline or look on a website. The same helplines and websites that help the targets of bullies can also help those doing the bullying themselves, and can give them advice on changing their behaviour.

Counselling can help the victims of bullying, and the bullies too.

It happened to me

Carly started bullying after her dad left home. She was miserable at home, and she hated the way her mum's new boyfriend kept picking on her. At school, Carly concentrated on bullying Gemma because she seemed to have everything. Carly decided that she wanted Gemma to feel just as bad as she did. Then, one day, Carly heard the news that Gemma had tried to kill herself. Carly was really frightened. She had never meant to go that far. When Gemma came back to school, Carly decided to stop persecuting her. Carly was surprised to find that when she stopped bullying, she actually felt better about herself.

Talking to each other

Some schools make an effort to bring bullies and their victims together. They arrange for all the people involved to meet in a safe environment with another person watching carefully. This process of meeting together and talking is known as mediation.

When bullies get to talk to their targets face-to-face, it can help them realize the real consequences of their actions.

Mediation gives people who have been bullied a chance to put across their point of view. It also allows the bullies to realize how much harm they have done. In some cases, a mediation session can end with the bully apologizing for their actions. It can mark the start of a much more positive pattern of behaviour. Mediation can be a great way to put an end to a painful situation. However, it is not suitable for all cases of bullying.

Chapter 7

Bullying in society

Sadly, bullying exists in all areas of society. There are bullies in families, in the workplace, and on the streets. Bullying happens whenever people try to threaten and frighten others. Fortunately, however, there are things that can be done to fight against and reduce bullying.

Some adults experience bullying and violence from their partners, and some adults are violent towards children in their home.

Bullying in the home

Many families experience some kind of bullying, as one family member attempts to frighten other people who share their home. Sometimes adult bullies target other adults in a family, but they can also turn on children. Young people can be subject to violence or to psychological abuse from adults. These experiences are especially frightening because the children cannot easily escape. Young people suffering from any form of bullying at home need help urgently. They should contact one of the helplines listed on page 47.

Bullying in the workplace

Many people suffer from bullying at work. Sometimes individuals can find that other people at work have ganged up against them and are sending cruel messages about them. It is also common for people to be deliberately excluded from groups at work. These experiences can make the workplace feel like a very threatening place. Bullying at work is often known as harassment, and it is against the law. Workers who are experiencing bullying need to take action to put a stop to it.

Violence on the streets

Modern society can be very violent, especially in our towns and cities. There are news reports of bullies in city streets, picking on innocent people. There are even some cases of unprovoked attacks. People from different races, disabled people and old people are especially at risk from name-calling, and even from violent attacks on the street.

In the media

In December 2005, Myleene Klass was attacked as she walked home from work.
A group of girls and two boys threatened to kill her, emptied a bag of chips on her head and flung her to the ground. Then they tried to photograph her on their mobile phones before they ran away.
Myleene belonged to the pop group Hear'say and she has worked as a TV presenter in the UK. Before the attack, she had launched the website 'Stop the Text Bully' because of her bad experiences with phone bullying when she was at school. After her frightening attack, Myleene was even more determined to put a stop to bullying.

Racism

Racism is bullying that is directed at people because of their race, their religion or the colour of their skin. There is never any excuse for racism and it causes great suffering. Racism takes place in schools, at work and on the streets. Many people work very hard to put a stop to racist bullying, but it is still a major problem in the world today. Every day, people are victimized because of their colour, religion or race.

When people have been victims of hate crimes, they need lots of support. Fortunately, there are organizations that provide help and counselling for victims.

Hate crimes

Hate crimes are another terrible form of bullying. They can range from attacks on people's property to murder. Hate crimes are usually carried out by groups in society against other groups who are seen as 'outsiders'.

People with different religions, refugees and homosexuals can all be victims of hate crimes. Governments have very strict punishments for people who plan or commit hate crimes.

TALK ABOUT

Some people say it is impossible to put a stop to bullying in society. They say that bullying is part of human nature and there will always be bullies. Other people believe that it is possible to change people's behaviour. They say that people can learn better ways to behave towards one another.

✳ Do you think that people can change?

Building a better world

There are many people in the world today who are determined to take a stand against bullying. Governments make laws to protect their citizens' freedom. Charities work hard to protect the rights of people at risk. There are also many publicity campaigns to make people aware of the problems of bullying and violence. Meanwhile, many people work as counsellors, helping the bullies and their targets.

All these positive actions help to tackle the problem. However, there is still a huge amount to do. What do you think should be done to help stop bullying in our society?

The photograph below shows an anti-racism march in Paris in 2006. Sixty thousand people gathered together in memory of Ilan Halimi, a young Jew who was killed by a gang.

Glossary

anorexia An eating disorder, in which people feel a powerful need to be thin. People with anorexia only allow themselves to eat tiny amounts of food. Anorexia is short for anorexia nervosa.

body language Showing your feelings through the way you use your body.

breakdown A complete collapse, caused by too much worry and stress. When people have a breakdown, they need help to recover.

chatrooms Internet sites where people can 'chat' to one another online.

cyberbullying Bullying that is carried out via computers or mobile phones.

eating disorder A mental health problem which causes people to develop an unhealthy attitude towards food.

excluded Kept out of school as a punishment.

hate crimes Violent attacks that are driven by a powerful hatred of a person or group of people.

homophobic bullying Bullying aimed at people who are homosexual or who are believed to be homosexual.

humiliating Making you feel ashamed.

in confidence Without letting anyone else know.

Internet Service Providers Organizations that provide people or businesses with access to the Internet. They are often called ISPs.

mediation A method of bringing people together so they can talk calmly about disagreements between them.

panic attack A sudden feeling of being very scared. When people suffer a panic attack, their heart beats very fast and they feel cold and sweaty.

persecute To treat people cruelly and unfairly because of prejudice.

psychological abuse Very cruel treatment, through words or behaviour. Psychological abuse does not involve physical violence but it can cause just as much damage.

school council A group set up to deal with problems in a school. School councils include representatives of the pupils and the staff.

self-harm Deliberately hurting yourself. Cutting is a form of self-harm.

suspended Kept out of school for a short time as punishment.

taunting Cruel teasing and name-calling, intended to make someone lose their temper.

verbally abusive Using cruel language, swear words and name-calling to attack someone.

victimize To pick someone out for unfair treatment.

vulnerable In a weak position.

workshop A meeting in which people act out different roles, to help them understand more about a problem.

Further information

Notes for Teachers:
The Talk About panels are to be used to encourage debate and avoid the polarization of views. One way of doing this is to use 'continuum lines'. Think of a range of statements or opinions about the topics that can then be considered by the pupils. An imaginary line is constructed that pupils can stand along to show what they feel in response to each statement (please see above). If they strongly agree or disagree with the viewpoint they can stand by the signs, if the response is somewhere in between they stand along the line in the relevant place. If the response is 'neither agree, nor disagree' or they 'don't know' then they stand at an equal distance from each sign, in the middle. Alternatively, continuum lines can be drawn out on paper and pupils can mark a cross on the line to reflect their views.

Books to read
It Happened To Me: Bullied by Angela Neustatter and Anastasia Gonis (Franklin Watts, 2008)

Bullies, Bigmouths and So-Called Friends by Jenny Alexander (Hodder, 2006)

Websites and Helplines
ChildLine
A free and confidential helpline for young people. ChildLine also has a very helpful website with a large section on bullying, including real-life stories.
Website:
www.childline.org.uk
Phone: 00 44 (0) 800 1111 (Free 24-hour helpline)

Kidscape
A charity founded specifically to prevent bullying and child abuse. The website contains clear advice on how to deal with bullying, including a section on cyberbullying.
Website:
www.kidscape.org.uk

Kids Help Line (Australia)
A confidential helpline for children and young people.
Website:
www.kidshelp.com.au

No More Bullies (Canada)
A site about bullying, its effects on young children and what can be done about it.
Website:
www.nfb.ca/webextension /nomorebullies/index.html

Champions Against Bullying
An interactive anti-bullying resource for children, parents and educators.
Website:
www.championsagainst bullying.com

Stop Bullying Now
A lively website about bullying and ways to prevent it.
Website:
www.stopbullying now.com

Index

TALK ABOUT

Contents of titles in the series:

Bullying

978 0 7502 4617 0
1. Let's talk about bullying
2. What is bullying?
3. How does it feel to be bullied?
4. Who gets bullied?
5. Why do people bully?
6. Beating bullying
7. Bullying in society

Eating Disorders and Body Image

978 0 7502 4936 2
1. What are eating disorders?
2. Food and the body
3. What does it mean to have an eating disorder?
4. Who gets eating disorders?
5. What causes eating disorders?
6. Preventing problems
7. The treatment of eating disorders

Racism

978 0 7502 4935 5
1. What is racism?
2. Why are people racist?
3. What do racists do?
4. Hidden racism
5. What is religious prejudice?
6. Racism against migrants
7. Nazi racial policies
8. What can we do about racism?

Drugs

978 0 7502 4937 9
1. What are drugs?
2. Why do we take drugs?
3. What about drinking and smoking?
4. What's the law on drugs?
5. What about cannabis?
6. What other drugs are there?
7. Paying the price
8. It's your choice

Homelessness

978 0 7502 4934 8
1. What is homelessness?
2. Why do people become homeless?
3. Homelessness and children
4. Addiction and homelessness
5. Staying clean and healthy
6. Mental health
7. Working and earning
8. Helping the homeless

Youth Crime

978 0 7502 4938 6
1. What is crime?
2. Crime past and present
3. Why does youth crime happen?
4. Behaving badly
5. Crimes of theft
6. Crimes of violence
7. What happens if you commit a crime?
8. What can you do about crime?

WAYLAND